BEAR'S PAW PLUS

Make New Tracks
with Sampler Blocks

Pat A. Syta

Martingale™
& COMPANY

Acknowledgments

The concept for this book started with the planning of Quilt Camp, a four-day quilting workshop which I co-sponsor with my friend Cheri Cooper. Trying to develop something interesting and new to teach, Cheri suggested I offer a couple of variations for the paw pads in Bear's Paw blocks. Later on, while sewing at an all-nighter, my friends Debbie Repasky and Sharon Swieter urged me to try new versions of the Bear's Paw block. After making four sampler blocks and having too much fun, I continued and made twelve sampler blocks for paw pads in Bear's Paw blocks. Debbie encouraged me to do something with my newfound design idea. Even after moving to Hawaii, Debbie continued encouraging me to pursue the dream—and this book is the end result.

Without many friends, my family, my outstanding students who sewed samples for this book, and the great folks at Martingale & Company, this book could not have happened. And I cannot forget Judy Dales, who gave me the final push when visiting my home. I am forever grateful.

Dedication

- To my special friends, Debbie and Cheri, and to Quilt Camp.

- To my loving husband, Stan, for letting me do my thing with quilting and not asking about all that fabric.

- To my sons—Dean, for his willingness to drop what he is doing and help me with countless hours of expert drafting; and Dale, for the many long-distance calls that always end with "I love you, Mom."

- To my Lord; praise to Him for His gifts bestowed on me—life, health, happiness, and a wonderful circle of family and friends.

Credits

President ◆ Nancy J. Martin
CEO ◆ Daniel J. Martin
Publisher ◆ Jane Hamada
Editorial Director ◆ Mary V. Green
Managing Editor ◆ Tina Cook
Technical Editor ◆ Dawn Anderson
Copy Editor ◆ Ellen Balstad
Design Director ◆ Stan Green
Illustrator ◆ Laurel Strand
Cover and Text Designer ◆ Regina Girard
Photographer ◆ Brent Kane

That Patchwork Place® is an imprint of Martingale & Company™

Bear's Paw Plus:
Make New Tracks with Sampler Blocks
© 2002 by Pat A. Syta

Martingale & Company
20205 144th Avenue NE
Woodinville, WA 98072-8478 USA
www.martingale-pub.com

Printed in China
07 06 05 04 03 02   8 7 6 5 4 3 2 1

Mission Statement

We are dedicated to providing quality products and service by working together to inspire creativity and to enrich the lives we touch.

Library of Congress Cataloging-In-Publication data available upon request.

ISBN: 1-56477-424-4

Contents

Introduction

The quilts in this book are made with Bear's Paw blocks, but they're not your traditional Bear's Paw blocks. These blocks are made with a unique twist, and that's why the book is called *Bear's Paw Plus*. Traditionally the paw pads on a 14" Bear's Paw block are made with 4" squares of fabric. The "plus" in my blocks is that I use identical 4" pieced blocks for the paw pads.

This book provides you with directions for 12 different pieced sampler blocks that you can choose from for the paw pads in the Bear's Paw blocks. You can make the quilts with the sampler blocks provided, or you can add one or more of your own favorite pieced blocks. Just remember that the pieced block needs to be 4" x 4" when finished (4½" x 4½" including seam allowances) to fit into the area for the paw pad.

Traditional Bear's Paw block

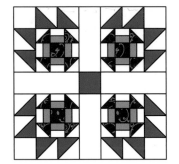

Bear's Paw Plus block

Rotary Cutting

For rotary cutting you need a rotary cutter, a cutting mat, and some acrylic rulers designed for use with a rotary cutter. These tools make it easy to cut your fabric quickly and accurately.

1. Press the wrinkles out of your fabric with small amounts of spray starch, if you prewashed the fabric. With wrong sides together, fold the fabric in half, selvage to selvage. With the selvages in your hands, hold the fabric up to see if it hangs straight. Slide the layers back and forth until the layers hang straight, and keep the selvages even at the top. Place the fabric on a cutting surface and align the fold with the selvages.

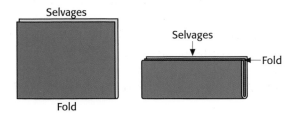

2. Align the bottom fold on a horizontal line on your cutting mat. Taking a 6" or 8" square ruler, line it up precisely with the bottom fold, about ½" from the left edge of the fabric. Make sure all 4 layers of fabric are under the ruler.

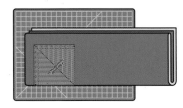

3. Line up your longest ruler tight against the left edge of the square ruler. Be sure there are 4 layers of fabric under the entire edge of the long ruler. Spread the fingertips of your left hand evenly and apply firm pressure on the long ruler, making sure your fingers are on the ruler and not hanging over the right edge. Remove the square ruler. Start with

your rotary cutter open and your blade on the mat about ½" before the bottom fold of fabric, keeping the blade firmly against the right edge of the ruler. Cut along the ruler edge, removing the uneven edges of fabric with just one cut. Immediately close your blade when you get to the top of the long ruler; make a habit of doing this. Rotary blades are extremely sharp and should be stored away from small children at all times. Always be careful and attentive when using a rotary cutter.

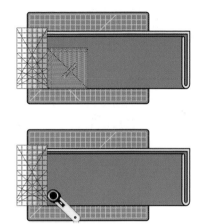

4. On your ruler, locate and line up the required pattern measurement with the straight-cut edge of the fabric. Measure twice and cut once. Cut the required strips, straightening the edge of the fabric if necessary by repeating steps 1–3.

5. Turn your strips of fabric, aligning them with the horizontal line on the cutting mat. Placing your long ruler on the left selvage edge of the fabric, align a horizontal line on your ruler with the horizontal edge of the fabric. Now check that your ruler is also aligned vertically with lines on the mat, and cut the selvage edge off the strips. Crosscut the strips into the squares or rectangles required in the project instructions.

Half-Square-Triangle Units

The projects in this book call for one of the most popular pieced units in quilting: half-square-triangle units, which are made up of two triangles whose short sides are on the straight grain. These triangles are generally cut from a square that is ⅞" larger than the finished size of the short edge of the triangle, hence the name half-square triangle. The units can be made by sewing two half-square triangles together.

Making Multiple Units

To speed the piecing process, I like to make several units at the same time whenever possible. With the introduction of half-square-triangle paper, the process for making multiple units is faster and more accurate. The projects in this book are made with half-square-triangle units that finish to 1" and 2", as well as 1⅓". However, half-square-triangle paper for the 1⅓" finished (1⅚" unfinished) size is not available. Because of the odd size, I have included a special pattern on page 47 for making multiple 1⅓" finished half-square-triangle units.

If the 1" or 2" half-square-triangle paper is not available at your local quilt shop or fabric store, follow the directions on page 6 for "Making Units *without* Triangle Paper."

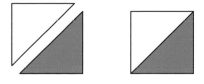

Making Units with Triangle Paper

1. Following the cutting directions for the project, cut rectangles or squares of fabric to make half-square-triangle units. Place contrasting fabric pieces right sides together. As indicated in the project instructions, pin the required number of squares of half-square-triangle paper, or a photocopy of the pattern on page 47 for the 1⅓" finished units, to the wrong side of the lighter fabric.

🐻 TIP 🐻

Use straight pins with flat heads to help prevent puckering of fabric and to keep the paper more flat. Change your sewing machine needle to a large topstitch or jeans needle and shorten your stitch length to 1.5mm or 15 stitches per inch. These changes help perforate the paper for easier removal after stitching.

2. Stitch on the dotted lines.

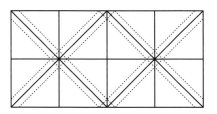

3. Cut away excess fabric around the edge of the paper; then cut on the solid lines. Tear off the paper. Hold your thumbnail between the stitching line and seam allowance. Grab the paper triangle with your other hand and pull paper away in one quick motion. With a little practice, this step goes very quickly. Press toward the darker fabric. Trim the "dog ears." Change your sewing machine needle back to your favorite size.

Trim "dog ears."

Making Units <u>without</u> Triangle Paper

1. Following the cutting directions included with the projects, cut rectangles or squares of fabric to make half-square-triangle units. Place contrasting fabric pieces right sides together.

2. On the wrong side of the lighter fabric, draw a grid of squares in the size required. For 1" finished units, your grid squares need to measure 1⅞" x 1⅞". For 1⅓" finished units, your grid squares need to measure 2¼" x 2¼". For 2" finished units, your grid squares need to measure 2⅞" x 2⅞".

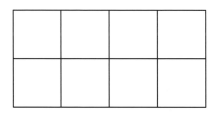

3. Draw a diagonal cutting line from corner to corner through each square in the grid.

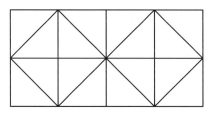

4. Stitch ¼" away from both sides of a diagonal cutting line. (For accuracy, you may want to draw the stitching lines before you stitch. Use a different color of marker to draw the stitching lines to distinguish them from the marked cutting line.) Repeat for all remaining squares.

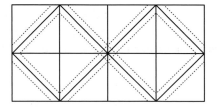

5. Cut on all marked cutting lines on the grid, using a rotary cutter and ruler. Remove the paper. Press carefully toward darker fabric. Trim the "dog ears."

Bear's Paw Block

Follow the directions below to make the Bear's Paw blocks. Use four identical sampler blocks for the paw pads. Refer to pages 7–19 to make the sampler blocks. Yardage requirements for the Bear's Paw blocks and sampler blocks are listed with each quilt project. Cutting directions for the Bear's Paw blocks (except for the sampler block paw pads) are listed with the projects.

1. Referring to "Half-Square-Triangle Units" on pages 5–6, make sixteen 2" finished units. Use the fabric rectangles or squares specified in your project.

2. Join 4 half-square-triangle units, one 2½" square, and 1 sampler block to make 1 quarter of a Bear's Paw block.

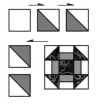

Make 4 identical
quarters for
each block.

3. Join 4 quarters, four 2½" x 6½" rectangles, and one 2½" contrasting square to make 1 Bear's Paw block.

 TIP

As you arrange the pieces for the Bear's Paw block, rotate the sampler blocks to see which way they look best. You may be surprised at the secondary pattern that is created in the center of the block. Also try changing the color of your 2½" center square to see what happens. By making these little changes, you personalize your quilt.

Sampler Blocks

The following section includes directions for making 12 different 4" sampler blocks, which can be used to replace the 4" square of fabric used for the paw pad in the traditional Bear's Paw block. Make 4 identical sampler blocks for each Bear's Paw block.

I *normally* assemble the pieces that make up a sampler block with a scant ¼" seam to allow for the extra threads that are taken up in the turn of the cloth when the seam allowance is pressed to one side. However, there are six sampler blocks—Churn Dash, Friendship Star, Tennessee Puzzle, Maple Leaf, Nine Patch, and Shoofly—that require using a generous ¼" seam allowance, rather than the scant ¼". These six sampler blocks are made with squares and rectangles that are cut slightly larger than necessary to avoid dimensions that are difficult to locate on a ruler.

For example, instead of cutting a 1⅚" square for the Churn Dash block, I cut a 1⅞" square. It's much easier to locate 1⅞" on my ruler than 1⅚". By stitching the pieces in these six sampler blocks with a *generous* ¼" seam rather than a scant ¼" seam, I am able to make sampler blocks that measure 4" and fit perfectly into the paw pad position of the Bear's Paw block.

Finally, to best use your fabric, first cut all pieces listed in the project instructions; then cut the fabric for the sampler blocks. The cutting instructions for the sampler blocks indicate specific fabrics to use for each location. The actual fabrics used, however, may vary in the individual quilt projects. Refer to the yardage requirements listed with each quilt project and the project photo for guidance with fabric placement. Feel free to substitute fabrics as desired.

Churn Dash

Cutting for Four 4" Blocks

From black print, cut:
- 1 rectangle, 5½" x 10¼"
- 4 squares, each 1⅞" x 1⅞"

From gold, cut:
- 1 strip, 1³⁄₁₆" x 34"

From white background, cut:
- 1 rectangle, 5½" x 10¼"
- 1 strip, 1³⁄₁₆" x 34"

Directions

Remember to use a generous ¼" seam allowance when sewing the pieces together for this block.

1. Referring to "Half-Square-Triangle Units" on pages 5–6, make sixteen 1⅓" finished half-square-triangle units. Use the black print and white rectangles.

Make 16.

Note: *For triangle paper, make 1 photocopy of the pattern on page 47.*

2. Join the 1³⁄₁₆" x 34" gold and white strips to make a strip set. Crosscut the strip set into 16 side segments, 1⅞" wide.

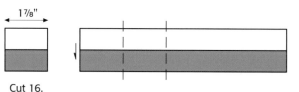

Cut 16.

3. Join 4 half-square-triangle units, 4 side segments, and a black print square to make 1 block.

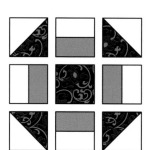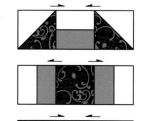

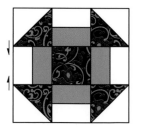

Make 4.

Friendship Star

Cutting for Four 4" Blocks

From black print, cut:
- 1 rectangle, 5½" x 10¼"

From gold, cut:
- 4 squares, each 1⅞" x 1⅞"

From white background, cut:
- 1 rectangle, 5½" x 10¼"
- 16 squares, each 1⅞" x 1⅞"

Directions

Remember to use a generous ¼" seam allowance when sewing the pieces together for this block.

1. Referring to "Half-Square-Triangle Units" on pages 5–6, make sixteen 1⅓" finished units. Use the black print and white rectangles.

Make 16.

Note: *For triangle paper, make 1 photocopy of the pattern on page 47.*

2. Join 4 half-square-triangle units, 4 white squares, and 1 gold square to make 1 block.

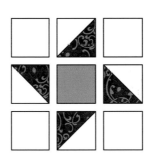

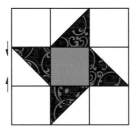

Make 4.

Old Maid's Puzzle

Cutting for Four 4" Blocks

From black print, cut:
- 4 squares, each 1⅞" x 1⅞"; cut squares once-diagonally to make 8 small triangles
- 4 squares, each 2⅞" x 2⅞"; cut squares once diagonally to make 8 large triangles

From gold, cut:
- 1 rectangle, 4¼" x 8"

From white background, cut:
- 16 squares, each 1½" x 1½"
- 12 squares, each 1⅞" x 1⅞"; cut squares once diagonally to make 24 small triangles
- 1 rectangle, 4¼" x 8"

Directions

1. Referring to "Half-Square-Triangle Units" on pages 5–6, make sixteen 1" finished units. Use the gold and white rectangles.

Make 16.

2. Join 2 half-square-triangle units and 2 white squares to make unit A.

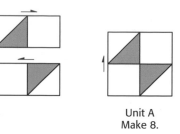

Unit A
Make 8.

3. Join 1 small black print triangle and 3 small white triangles to make unit B.

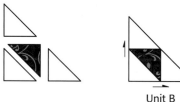

Unit B
Make 8.

4. Join a large black print triangle and a unit B to make unit C.

Unit C
Make 8.

5. Join 2 of unit A and 2 of unit C to make 1 block.

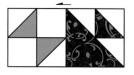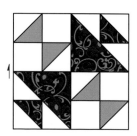

Make 4.

Tennessee Puzzle

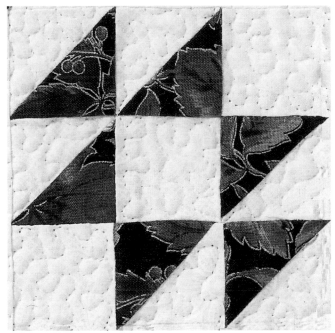

Directions

Remember to use a generous ¼" seam allowance when sewing the pieces together for this block.

1. Referring to "Half-Square-Triangle Units" on pages 5–6, make twenty-four 1⅓" finished units. Use the black print and white rectangles.

Make 24.

Note: *For triangle paper, make 2 photocopies of the pattern on page 47, tape the copies together, and trim them to make a 12-square grid.*

2. Join 6 half-square-triangle units and 3 white squares to make 1 block.

Cutting for Four 4" Blocks

From black print, cut:
- 1 rectangle, 5½" x 15"

From white background, cut:
- 1 rectangle, 5½" x 15"
- 12 squares, each 1⅞" x 1⅞"

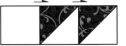

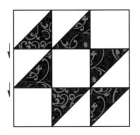

Make 4.

Birds in Flight

Cutting for Four 4" Blocks

From black print, cut:
- 1 rectangle, 6½" x 8½"

From red, cut:
- 8 squares, each 1½" x 1½"

From dark green, cut:
- 4 squares, each 2½" x 2½"

From white background, cut:
- 1 rectangle, 6½" x 8½"
- 4 squares, each 2½" x 2½"

Directions

1. Referring to "Half-Square-Triangle Units" on pages 5–6, make twenty-four 1" finished units. Use the black print and white rectangles.

Make 24.

2. Join 3 half-square-triangle units and a red square.

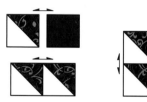

Make 8.

3. Join 2 units from step 2, a dark green square, and a white square to make 1 block.

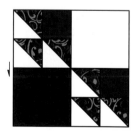

Make 4.

Maple Leaf

Cutting for Four 4" Blocks

From black print, cut:
- 1 rectangle, 5½" x 15"
- 4 squares, each 1⅞" x 1⅞"

From white background, cut:
- 1 rectangle, 5½" x 15"
- 8 squares, each 1⅞" x 1⅞"

Directions

Remember to use a generous ¼" seam allowance when sewing the pieces together for this block.

1. Referring to "Half-Square-Triangle Units" on pages 5–6, make twenty-four 1⅓" finished units. Use the black print and white rectangles.

Make 24.
Press 16 toward dark.
Press 8 toward light.

Note: *For triangle paper, make 2 photocopies of the pattern on page 47, tape the copies together, and trim them to make a 12-square grid.*

2. Join 6 half-square-triangle units, 1 black print square, and 2 white squares to make 1 block. Be sure seams of the triangle units are positioned as shown so that opposing seams create perfect points when the pieces are sewn together.

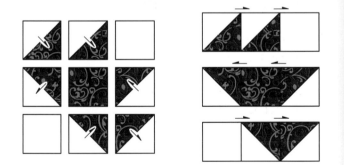

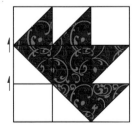

Make 4.

Nine Patch

Directions

Remember to use a generous ¼" seam allowance when sewing the pieces together for this block.

Join 1 black print square, 4 red squares, and 4 white squares to make 1 block.

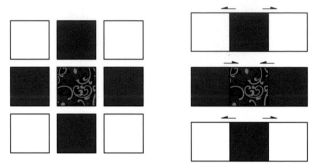

Make 4.

Cutting for Four 4" Blocks

From black print, cut:
- 4 squares, each 1⅞" x 1⅞"

From red, cut:
- 16 squares, each 1⅞" x 1⅞"

From white background, cut:
- 16 squares, each 1⅞" x 1⅞"

Sawtooth Star

Directions

1. Draw a diagonal line on the wrong side of the red squares. Place a red square on one end of a white rectangle, with right sides together. Sew on the diagonal line. Trim ¼" from the stitching line. Repeat with another square at the other end of the rectangle.

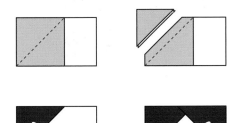

Make 16.

Cutting for Four 4" Blocks

From black print, cut:
- 4 squares, each 2½" x 2½"

From red, cut:
- 32 squares, each 1½" x 1½"

From white background, cut:
- 16 squares, each 1½" x 1½"
- 16 rectangles, each 1½" x 2½"

2. Join 4 units from step 1, 4 white squares, and 1 black print square to make 1 block.

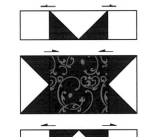

Make 4.

Shoofly

Cutting for Four 4" Blocks

From black print, cut:
- 1 rectangle, 5½" x 10¼"
- 4 squares, each 1⅞" x 1⅞"

From white background, cut:
- 1 rectangle, 5½" x 10¼"
- 16 squares, each 1⅞" x 1⅞"

Directions

Remember to use a generous ¼" seam allowance when sewing the pieces together for this block.

1. Referring to "Half-Square-Triangle Units" on pages 5–6, make sixteen 1⅓" finished units. Use the black print and white rectangles.

Make 16.

Note: *For triangle paper, make 1 photocopy of the pattern on page 47.*

2. Join 4 half-square-triangle units, 1 black print square, and 4 white squares to make 1 block.

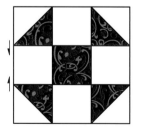

Make 4.

Railroad Crossing

Cutting for Four 4" Blocks

From gold, cut:
- 1 strip, 1½" x 26"

From red, cut:
- 4 squares, each 2⅞" x 2⅞"; cut the squares once diagonally to make 8 triangles

From white background, cut:
- 4 squares, each 2⅞" x 2⅞"; cut the squares once diagonally to make 8 triangles
- 1 strip, 1½" x 26"

Directions

1. With a scant ¼" seam, sew the 1½" x 26" gold and white strips together. Crosscut the strip set into 16 segments, each 1½" wide.

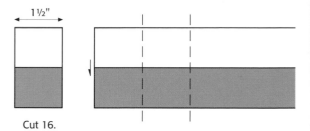

Cut 16.

2. Join 2 segments from step 1 to make a four-patch unit.

Make 0.

3. Join a red triangle and a white triangle on the long edges to make a half-square-triangle unit.

Make 8.

4. Join 2 half-square-triangle units, and 2 four-patch units to make 1 block.

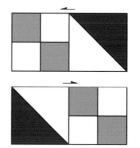 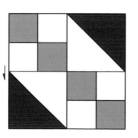

Make 4.

Yankee Puzzle

Directions

1. Referring to "Half-Square-Triangle Units" on pages 5–6, make sixteen 1" finished units, using the black print and white rectangles. Repeat, pairing a white rectangle with each of the gold, red, and dark green rectangles.

Make 16. Make 16. Make 16. Make 16.

2. For each of the 4 fabric colors, join 4 half-square-triangle units. Be sure seam allowances of units are pressed in the direction of the arrows.

Make 4
of each fabric color.

3. Join the units from step 2, using 1 of each color to make 1 block.

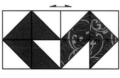
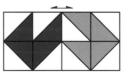
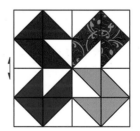

Make 4.

Cutting for Four 4" Blocks

From black print, cut:
- 1 rectangle, 4¼" x 8"

From gold, cut:
- 1 rectangle, 4¼" x 8"

From red, cut:
- 1 rectangle, 4¼" x 8"

From dark green, cut:
- 1 rectangle, 4¼" x 8"

From white background, cut:
- 4 rectangles, each 4¼" x 8"

Log Cabin

Cutting for Four 4" Blocks

From black print, cut:
- 1 strip, 1" x 42"

From gold, cut:
- 1 strip, 1" x 22"

From red, cut:
- 4 squares, each 1½" x 1½"

From dark green, cut:
- 1 strip, 1" x 26"

From white background, cut:
- 2 strips, each 1" x 42"

Directions

1. With right sides together, sew 4 red squares to one of the white strips; leave a tiny bit of space between the squares. Cut the units apart, trimming the strip even with the squares.

2. Sew the units from step 1 to a gold strip, with right sides together and white at the top. Cut the units apart, trimming the strip even with the pieced units.

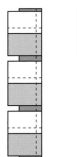

3. Sew the units from step 2 to the remaining gold strip, with right sides together and the last strip added at the top. Cut the units apart, trimming the strip even with the pieced units.

4. Sew the units from step 3 to a white strip, with right sides together and the last strip added at the top. Cut the units apart, trimming the strip even with the pieced units.

Note: Use the second white strip when you've used up the first one.

5. Continue in the same manner, adding dark green, white, and black print strips and ending with a white strip. Press the seams toward the strip just added, or away from the center square.

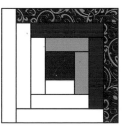

Make 4.

Adding Borders

For best results, do not cut border strips and sew them directly to the quilt sides without measuring first. The edges of a quilt often measure slightly longer than the distance through the quilt center, due to stretching during construction. Measure the quilt top through the center in both directions to determine how long to cut the border strips. This step ensures that the finished quilt will be as straight and as square as possible, without wavy edges.

The quilts in this book all have plain borders. The strips for borders can be cut from the crosswise grain (and seamed where extra length is needed), or from the lengthwise grain. Borders cut from the lengthwise grain require extra yardage, but seaming to achieve the required length is then unnecessary. Follow the steps below for adding borders.

1. Measure the width of the quilt top through the center. Cut border strips to that measurement, piecing as necessary. Mark the center of the quilt edges and the border strips. Pin the borders to the top and bottom edges of the quilt top, matching the center marks and ends and easing as necessary. Sew the border strips in place. Press seams toward the border.

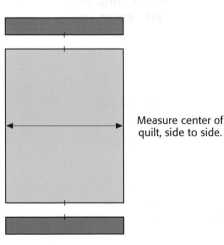

Measure center of quilt, side to side.

Mark centers.

2. Measure the length of the quilt top through the center, including the borders just added. Cut border strips to that measurement, piecing as necessary. Mark the center of the quilt edges and the border strips. Pin the borders to the side edges of the quilt top, matching the center marks and ends and easing as necessary; stitch. Press seams toward the border.

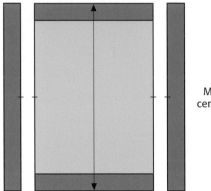

Mark centers.

Measure center of quilt, top to bottom, including borders.

The binding will complete and enclose the edges of your quilt. The patterns in this book give you the binding cutting directions for each project. If possible, use a walking foot to sew the binding to the quilt.

1. Measure the 4 outer edges of your quilt and add these amounts together; then add 10" to determine the total amount of binding you will need. Divide the total binding amount by 42" (the width of your fabric). Cut this number (binding divided by 42") of strips.

2. Using a diagonal seam, piece all strips together to form a long strip. Trim the excess fabric from the diagonal seams and press the seams open.

3. Turn one end of the binding under at a 45° angle. Now fold the binding strip in half lengthwise, with wrong sides together; press.

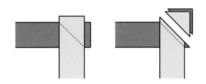

Fold line

4. Working from the front of your quilt and with the binding end that you turned under, pin the binding to the quilt about halfway along one edge. With a ¼" seam allowance, start sewing about 2" from where you first pinned the binding. Sew to ¼" from the first corner.

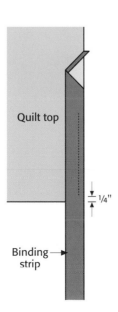

Quilt top

¼"

Binding strip

5. Leaving the needle down in the quilt, pivot the quilt to the right and backstitch to the raw edge of the quilt. Your binding should be at the top of the quilt and the next edge you will sew is to the right or in front of the needle. Lift the presser foot up but keep the needle in the edge of the fabric.

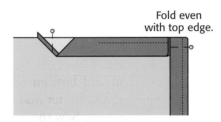

6. Fold the binding up and then down so that the fold is even with the top edge of the quilt. Put the presser foot down and begin stitching again with a ¼" seam allowance.

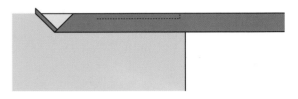

Fold even with top edge.

7. Continue stitching until you reach the next corner and repeat the process described in steps 5–6. When you have sewn all the way around the quilt top and come near the beginning binding tail, stop and trim the end of the binding so that it is just long enough to tuck into the beginning tail. Open the beginning tail and tuck in the end of the binding. Pin in place and stitch.

8. Turn the folded edge of the binding to the back of the quilt, making sure your binding is smooth and covers the stitching on the back. Blindstitch the binding to the back of the quilt. Fold the corners to form a nice miter, adding a stitch or two to keep the corners from popping out.

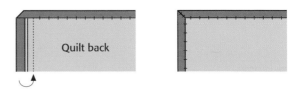

Quilt back

Gallery

Bear's Paws in the Garden

By Marianne Strahle, 100" x 122". Quilted by Maret Anderson.

Marianne used pansy fabric with greens, and a marbled background fabric to make this inviting quilt. Maret's wonderful wreath and feather quilting add that extra class!

River of Dreams

By Opal Hoffman, 80" x 98".

Hubby Dan enjoys and cherishes Opal's gift to him. The sashing fabric reminds Dan year-round of his favorite Alaskan pastime—fishing!

Bear's Paws at Play

By Mary Downs, 102" x 121".
Quilted by Norma Kindred.

You can't help but say "Wow" when looking at the spectacular array of colors Mary has introduced into this sampler. With Norma's expert quilting designs, the quilt is one to treasure.

Paw Prints of Multicultural Bears

By Rhonda Orth, 76¾" x 76¾".

Rhonda was one of the first "test pilots" for the pattern and her quilt won a blue ribbon at the "Quilting on the Kenai" show. Her choice of batik fabrics makes the mood of the quilt change in different lighting.

Bears in My Yard

By Sharon Swieter, 96" x 120". Quilted by Maret Anderson.

Working with scraps is Sharon's passion; she and Maret accomplished a beautiful job here. Sharon mixed traditional Bear's Paw blocks with the new sampler blocks.

Blazing Paws

By Michelle Fischer, 44" x 60".
Quilted by Tracey Bunts.

Michelle made this quilt as a gift for a friend. Her warmth in sharing is extended through the great fall colors used in this gift.

Bear's Paw Kokopelli

By Leslie Glasgow, 96" x 116".
Quilted by Maret Anderson.

Leslie grew up in the Southwest and stays connected through this quilt, which uses great southwestern patterned fabric along with turquoise and rust colors. Leslie designed the patterns that Maret quilted, continuing the flair with Kokopelli figures, cactus, howling wolves, prairie grass, and symbols.

Different Paws of Bears

By Pat A. Syta. Quilted by Mary Johnson.

This breathtaking quilt resulted when I combined my design of Bear's Paw sampler blocks with Mary's outstanding quilting.

Finished Quilt Size: 96½" x 122"
Finished Block Size: 14" x 14"

Materials

Yardage requirements are based on 42" wide fabric unless otherwise stated.

4 yds. dark fabric 1 (fabric A) for sampler blocks, center squares in Bear's Paw blocks, sashing, and three-dimensional flying geese in border

½ yd. light fabric (fabric B) for sampler blocks

4 yds. medium fabric (fabric C) for sampler blocks, star cornerstones, inner and outer borders, and binding

1¼ yds. dark fabric 2 (fabric D) for toes in Bear's Paw blocks and sampler blocks

7¼ yds. light background fabric (fabric E)

8½ yds. for backing

King-size batting

Cutting Directions

To best use your fabric, first cut all fabric pieces as listed below; then cut the fabrics for the sampler blocks as indicated on pages 7–19. All measurements include ¼"-wide seam allowances.

From fabric A, cut:
- 48 rectangles, each 4½" x 14½", for star-point sashing strips
- 120 rectangles, each 2½" x 4½", for three-dimensional flying geese in middle border
- 12 squares, each 2½" x 2½", for center squares in Bear's Paw blocks

From fabric C, cut:
- 31 squares, each 4½" x 4½", for star centers
- 192 squares, each 2½" x 2½", for star points
- 20 strips, each 2" x 42", for inner and outer borders
- 11 strips, each 2¼" x 42", for binding

From fabric D, cut:
- 12 rectangles, each 7" x 12", for toes in Bear's Paw blocks

From fabric E, cut:
- 3 squares, each 27" x 27"; cut the squares twice diagonally to make 12 side setting triangles. You will have 2 left over.
- 6 squares, each 14½" x 14½", for alternate blocks
- 2 squares, each 17" x 17"; cut the squares once diagonally to make 4 corner setting triangles
- 240 squares, each 2½" x 2½", for three-dimensional flying geese in middle border
- 4 rectangles, each 4½" x 13", for middle border
- 4 rectangles, each 4½" x 25¾", for middle border
- 4 squares, each 4½" x 4½", for corner squares of middle border
- 48 rectangles, each 2½" x 6½", for Bear's Paw blocks
- 48 squares, each 2½" x 2½", for Bear's Paw blocks
- 12 rectangles, each 7" x 12", for toes in Bear's Paw blocks

Blocks

1. Make 4 each of the 12 sampler blocks on pages 7–19. You may also use just one of your favorite sampler block designs, if desired. If you use different sampler blocks from those shown, the yardage requirements may vary.

2. Following the instructions for "Bear's Paw Block" (page 7), construct 12 Bear's Paw blocks. Use the 7" x 12" fabric D and fabric E rectangles for the toes. Use 4 identical sampler blocks for each Bear's Paw block.

Three-Dimensional Flying Geese

1. Fold a 2½" x 4½" fabric A rectangle in half, wrong sides together. Place the folded rectangle between two 2½" fabric E squares, right sides together with bottom and side raw edges aligned. The folded edge of the rectangle will be approximately ¼" below the top edge of the sandwich.

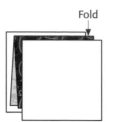

Fold

2. With bottom edges aligned, sew a ¼" seam on the right-hand side.

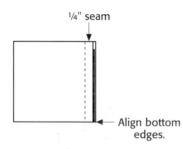

¼" seam

Align bottom edges.

3. Open the 2 fabric E squares. Position the fold in the rectangle center over the seam line, creating a triangle. Align the raw edges at the lower edge; press. The point of the triangle should be ¼" away from the top edge of the flying-geese unit.

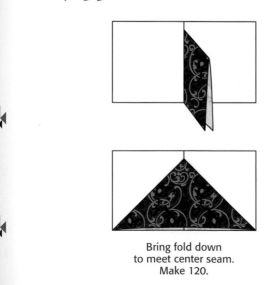

Bring fold down to meet center seam.
Make 120.

Star-Point Sashing Strips

Draw a diagonal line from corner to corner on the wrong sides of all 2½" fabric C squares. Place a fabric C square over each upper corner of a 4½" x 14½" fabric A rectangle, right sides together. Sew on the marked lines. Trim ¼" from the stitching. Repeat on the lower corners of the rectangle to make a star-point sashing strip.

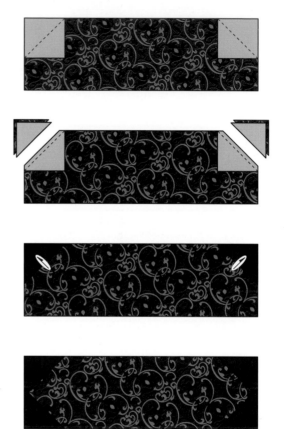

Make 48.

Assembly and Finishing

1. Join a Bear's Paw block, 2 star-point sashing strips, and a 4½" fabric C square. Repeat with the 14½" fabric E alternate blocks.

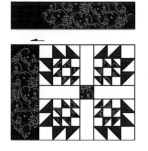

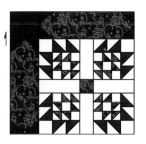

Make 12.

Make 6.

2. Join a 4¼" fabric C square to the left side of the remaining star-point sashing strips.

Make 12.

3. Arrange the blocks on point, and add star-point sashing units and side triangles as shown.

4. Join the blocks and side triangles in diagonal rows to make 2 halves.

5. Join 6 star-point sashing units and a 4½" fabric C square at the end on the right.

6. Sew the long sashing strip between the 2 halves as shown at right. Add the corner triangles last.

7. Trim the edges of the quilt ¼" away from all points, and square up corners if necessary.

8. Referring to "Adding Borders" (page 20), prepare the inner border strips and sew them to the top and bottom edges of the quilt top first; then sew the strips to the side edges. Press the seams toward the border.

9. Make a total of 12 flying-geese border strips, joining 10 flying-geese units in 2 different arrangements.

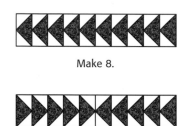

Make 8.

Make 4.

10. Join the flying-geese border strips and the fabric E rectangles to make the middle borders, adding the 4½" fabric E squares to each end of the side borders. You may need to adjust your seam allowances or the length of the rectangles to make the borders fit.

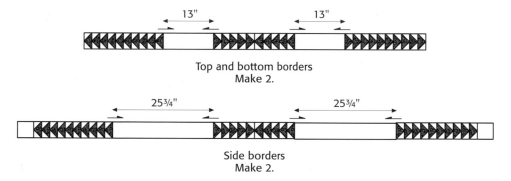

13"   13"

Top and bottom borders
Make 2.

25¾"   25¾"

Side borders
Make 2.

11. Sew the middle border strips to the top and bottom edges of the quilt top first; then sew the strips to the side edges. Press the seams toward the inner border.

12. Referring to "Adding Borders" (page 20), prepare the outer border strips and sew them to the top and bottom edges of the quilt top first; then sew the strips to the side edges. Press the seams toward the outer border.

13. Layer the pieced top with backing and batting; baste. Quilt as desired.

14. Bind the edges and add a label.

Bear's Paws with Nine Patches

By Debbie Repasky. Quilted by Maret Anderson.

Debbie, who inspired me to pursue my dream of writing a book,
willingly created this cheerful wall hanging when asked to help.

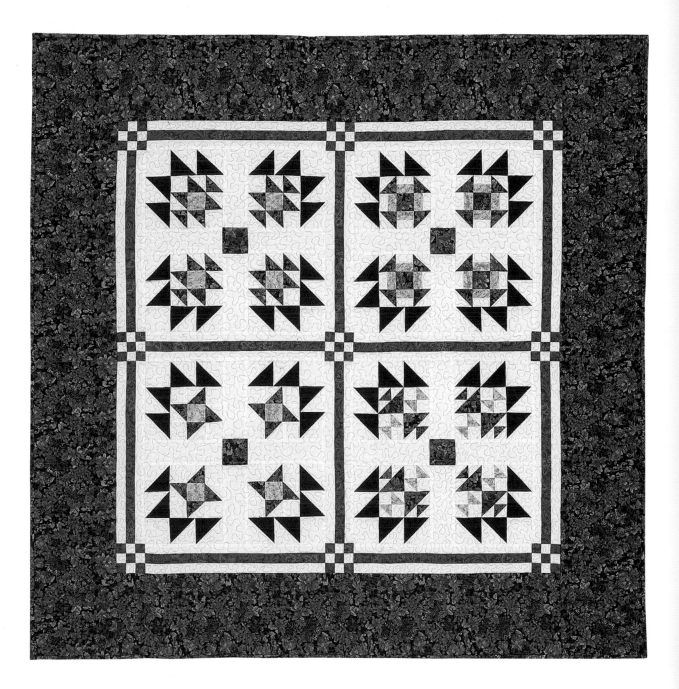

Finished Quilt Size: 47¾" x 47¾"
Finished Block Size: 14" x 14"

Materials

Yardage requirements are based on 42"-wide fabric unless otherwise stated.

1⅔ yds. medium fabric 1 (fabric A) for sampler blocks, center squares in Bear's Paw blocks, borders, and binding

¼ yd. light fabric (fabric B) for sampler blocks

½ yd. dark fabric (fabric C) for toes in Bear's Paw blocks

1¾ yds. light background fabric (fabric D)

⅓ yd. medium fabric 2 (fabric E) for triple rail sashing and Nine Patch cornerstones

3 yds. for backing

54" x 54" piece of batting

Cutting Directions

To best use your fabric, first cut all fabric pieces as listed below; then cut the fabrics for the sampler blocks as indicated on pages 7–19. All measurements include ¼"-wide seam allowances.

From fabric A, cut from the lengthwise grain:
- 2 strips, 7" x 35¼", for borders
- 2 strips, 7" x 48¼", for borders
- 4 strips, 2¼" x 52", for binding
- 4 squares, 2½" x 2½", for center squares in Bear's Paw blocks

From fabric C, cut:
- 4 rectangles, 7" x 12", for toes in Bear's Paw blocks

From fabric D, cut:
- 12 strips, 1¼" x 42", for triple rail sashing
- 16 rectangles, 2½" x 6½", for Bear's Paw blocks
- 4 rectangles, 7" x 12", for toes in Bear's Paw blocks
- 16 squares, 2½" x 2½", for Bear's Paw blocks

From fabric E, cut:
- 6 strips, 1¼" x 42", for triple rail sashing and Nine Patch cornerstones
- 2 strips, 1¼" x 14", for triple rail sashing and Nine Patch cornerstones

Blocks

1. Make 4 each of the following blocks: Churn Dash (page 8), Friendship Star (page 9), Old Maid's Puzzle (page 10), and Tennessee Puzzle (page 11). Or choose your favorite sampler blocks and make 4 of each one. If you use different sampler blocks from those shown, the yardage requirements may vary.

2. Following the instructions for "Bear's Paw Block" (page 7), construct 4 blocks. Use the 7" x 12" fabric C and fabric D rectangles for the toes. Use 4 identical sampler blocks for each Bear's Paw block.

Triple Rail Sashing

1. Join 1¼" x 42" fabric D and fabric E strips to make 6 of strip set A. Cut 2 segments, each 14½" long, from each strip set for a total of 12 segments.

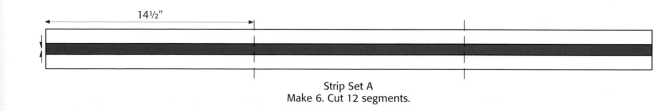

14½"

Strip Set A
Make 6. Cut 12 segments.

2. From 1 leftover strip set A portion, cut 9 segments, each 1¼" wide.

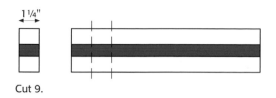

Cut 9.

3. From another 2 leftover strip set A portions, remove a fabric D strip; discard. Then sew 1¼" x 14" fabric E strips to the strip sets to make 2 of strip set B.

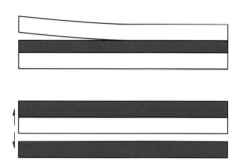

4. From strip set B, cut 18 segments, 1¼" wide.

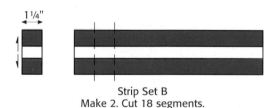

Strip Set B
Make 2. Cut 18 segments.

5. Join one 1¼"-wide strip set A segment and two 1¼"-wide strip set B segments to make a Nine Patch block.

Make 9.

6. Join two 14½" strip set A segments and 3 Nine Patch blocks to make a sashing row.

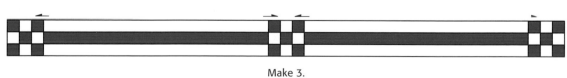

Make 3.

Assembly and Finishing

1. Join the Bear's Paw blocks into 2 rows of 2 blocks with a 14½" strip set A segment between the blocks and at the ends of the rows.

2. Join the 2 rows of blocks with a sashing row between and at the top and bottom.

3. Referring to "Adding Borders" (page 20), prepare the border strips and sew them to the top and bottom edges of the quilt top first; then sew the strips to the side edges.

4. Layer the pieced top with batting and backing; baste. Quilt as desired.

5. Add a hanging sleeve if desired. Bind the edges and add a label.

Mama's Bear's Paw

By Megan Ryan. Quilted by Maret Anderson.

This queen-size quilt project is a straight-set quilt with a scrappy look.
Megan made this quilt as a gift for her mother.

Finished Quilt Size: 86½" x 104½"
Finished Block Size: 14" x 14"

Materials

Yardage requirements are based on 42"-wide fabric unless otherwise stated.

6 or more fat quarters of light to medium-dark fabrics (fabric A) for sampler blocks

1⅝ yds. dark fabric (fabric B) for inner border, binding, and sampler blocks

1¾ yds. medium fabric 1 (fabric C) for star cornerstones and sampler blocks

3½ yds. medium fabric 2 (fabric D) for toes and center squares in Bear's Paw blocks, outer borders, and sampler blocks

7¾ yds. light background fabric (fabric E)

King-size batting

Cutting

To best use your fabric, first cut all fabric pieces as listed below; then cut the fabrics for the sampler blocks as indicated on pages 7–19. All measurements include ¼"-wide seam allowances.

From fabric B, cut:
- 7 strips, each 2½" x 42", for inner border
- 10 strips, each 2¼" x 42", for binding

From fabric C, cut:
- 20 squares, each 4½" x 4½", for star centers
- 160 squares, each 2½" x 2½", for star points

From fabric D, cut:
- 12 rectangles, each 7" x 12", for toes in Bear's Paw blocks
- 12 squares, each 2½" x 2½", for center squares in Bear's Paw blocks
- 8 strips, each 10½" x 42", for outer borders

From fabric E, cut:
- 31 rectangles, each 4½" x 14½", for sashing
- 14 rectangles, each 2½" x 14½", for outer-sashing edge
- 12 rectangles, each 7" x 12", for toes in Bear's Paw blocks
- 18 rectangles, each 2½" x 4½", for outer-sashing edge
- 48 rectangles, each 2½" x 6½", for Bear's Paw blocks
- 52 squares, each 2½" x 2½", for Bear's Paw blocks and outer-sashing edge

Sampler Blocks

1. Make 4 each of the 12 sampler blocks on pages 7–19. You may also use just one of your favorite sampler block designs, if desired. If you use different sampler blocks from those shown, the yardage requirements may vary. Megan repeated a few of her favorite sampler blocks and created a new one, Baby Bear; see page 36 if you wish to use it in place of one of the other sampler blocks.

2. Following the instructions for "Bear's Paw Block" (page 7), construct 12 blocks. Use the 7" x 12" fabric D and fabric E rectangles for the toes. Use 4 identical sampler blocks for each Bear's Paw block.

Baby Bear

Cutting for Four 4" Blocks

From medium-dark fabric (fabric A), cut:
- 1 rectangle, 5½" x 10¼"
- 4 squares, 3¼" x 3¼"

From light background fabric (fabric E), cut:
- 1 rectangle, 5½" x 10¼"
- 4 squares, 1⅞" x 1⅞"

Directions

Use a generous ¼" seam allowance when sewing the pieces together for this block.

1. Referring to "Half-Square-Triangle Units" on pages 5–6, make sixteen 1⅓" finished half-square-triangle units. Use the 5½" x 10¼" rectangles of fabric A and fabric E.

Make 16.

2. Join 4 half-square-triangle units, 1 small fabric E square, and 1 large fabric A square to make 1 block.

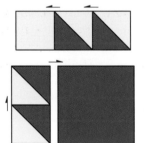 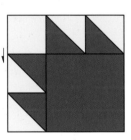

Make 4.

Star-Point Sashing

Draw a diagonal line from corner to corner on the wrong side of the 2½" fabric C squares. Place a fabric C square on each upper corner of a 4½" x 14½" fabric E rectangle, right sides together. Sew on the marked lines. Trim ¼" from the stitching. Repeat with a square on each lower corner of the rectangles to make the star-point sashing strips.

Make 31.

Assembly and Finishing

1. Join 2 star-point sashing strips, a 4½" fabric C square, and a Bear's Paw block.

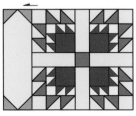 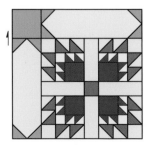

Make 12.

2. Arrange the joined Bear's Paw blocks and star-point sashing strips into 4 horizontal rows of 3 blocks each. Join the blocks into rows; then join the rows.

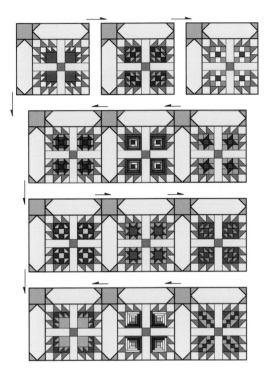

3. Join star-point sashing strips and 4½" fabric C squares as shown to make the sashing strips for the bottom and right edges of the quilt.

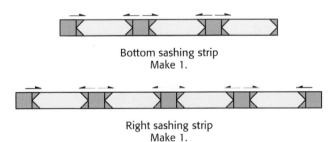

Bottom sashing strip
Make 1.

Right sashing strip
Make 1.

4. Join the bottom sashing strip and then the right sashing strip to the quilt top, matching the seam lines. Press the seams toward the sashing strips.

5. Draw a diagonal line from corner to corner on the wrong side of thirty-six 2½" fabric C squares. Place a fabric C square at one end of a 2½" x 4½" fabric E rectangle, right sides together. Sew on the marked line. Trim ¼" from the stitching. Repeat with a square on the other end of the rectangle.

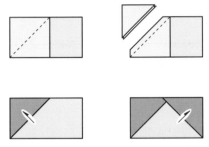

Make 18.

6. Join the units from step 5 and the 2½" x 14½" fabric E strips to make the outer-sashing edge strips, adding the 2½" fabric E squares to each end of the strips for the side as shown below.

7. Join the outer-sashing edge strips to the top and bottom edges of the quilt top first; then add the strips to the side edges. Press the seams toward the sashing.

8. Referring to "Adding Borders" on page 20, prepare the inner border strips and sew them to the top and bottom edges of the quilt top first; then sew the strips to the side edges. Repeat for the outer border.

9. Layer the pieced top with backing and batting; baste. Quilt as desired.

10. Bind the edges and add a label.

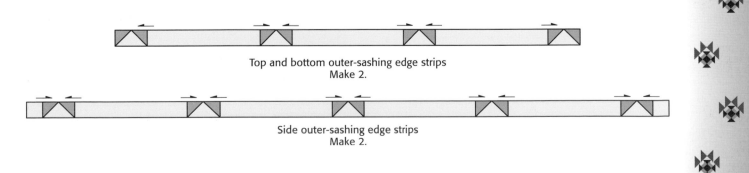

Top and bottom outer-sashing edge strips
Make 2.

Side outer-sashing edge strips
Make 2.

When Bears Come to Dinner

By Pat A. Syta.

Decorate your table with this dramatic table runner and four matching place mats.

Finished Table Runner Size: 26" x 71¼"
Finished Place Mat Size: 18" x 18"
Finished Block Size: 14" x 14"

Materials for Table Runner

Yardage requirements are based on 42"-wide fabric unless otherwise stated.

¾ yd. dark fabric (fabric A) for sampler blocks, toes and center squares in Bear's Paw blocks, and sashing

2 fat quarters medium fabric (fabrics B and C) for sampler blocks

2 fat quarters medium-dark fabric (fabric D) for sampler blocks

⅔ yd. light background fabric (fabric E)

2⅛ yds. for backing

31" x 76" piece of batting

Cutting Directions for Table Runner

To best use your fabric, first cut all fabric pieces as listed below; then cut the fabrics for the sampler blocks as indicated on pages 7–19. All measurements include ¼"-wide seam allowances.

From fabric A, cut:
- 12 strips, each 2½" x 14½", for sashing on large blocks
- 8 strips, each 2½" x 4½", for sashing on small blocks
- 3 squares, each 2½" x 2½", for center squares of Bear's Paw blocks
- 3 rectangles, each 7" x 12", for toes in Bear's Paw blocks

From fabric E, cut:
- 12 rectangles, each 2½" x 6½", for Bear's Paw blocks
- 3 rectangles, each 7" x 12", for toes in Bear's Paw blocks
- 26 squares, each 2½" x 2½", for Bear's Paw blocks and sashing

Blocks for Table Runner

1. Make 4 each of the following blocks: Churn Dash (page 8), Maple Leaf (page 13), Sawtooth Star (page 15), and Yankee Puzzle (page 18). In place of the 4 sampler block designs used here, you may substitute any of the sampler blocks found on pages 7–19. Or choose your favorite sampler block design and use it for all of the Bear's Paw blocks and the connecting blocks. If you use different sampler blocks from those shown, the yardage requirements may vary.

2. Following the instructions for "Bear's Paw Block" (page 7), construct 3 blocks. Use the 7" x 12" fabric A and fabric E rectangles for the toes. Select one set of blocks for the connecting blocks. Use 4 identical sampler blocks for each Bear's Paw block.

Assembly and Finishing for Table Runner

1. Join two 2½" x 14½" fabric A rectangles to opposite sides of each Bear's Paw block.

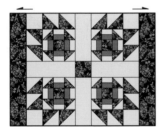

Make 3.

2. Join the 2½" fabric E squares and 2½" x 14½" fabric A rectangles to make two different sets of sashing strips.

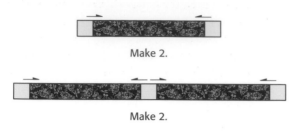

Make 2.

Make 2.

3. For the connecting blocks, join a sampler block, two 2½" x 4½" fabric A rectangles, and one 2½" fabric E square.

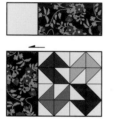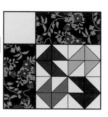

Make 4.

4. Join the connecting blocks to the sashed Bear's Paw blocks.

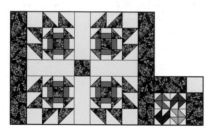

Make 2.

Make 1.

Where connecting blocks are stitched to longer sashing strips, clip the seam allowances about 1" in from the end of the block unit. Press the seam allowances toward the sashing on the block side of the clip mark. Press the seam allowance to the outside on the other side of the clip mark, so the seam allowances lie flat and the backing can be joined easily to the pieced top.

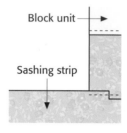

Block unit

Sashing strip

5. Arrange the block units and sashing strips on the diagonal as shown. Join the block units and sashing strips together.

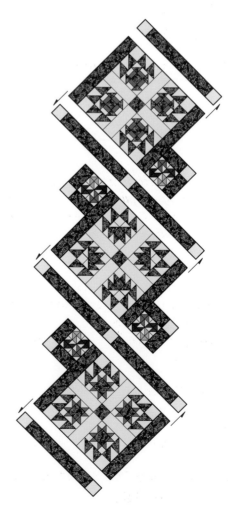

6. Layer batting, backing, and the pieced table-runner top on your work surface, right sides together. Pin-baste the layers together and stitch ¼" from all edges, leaving a 5" opening on one side of the center Bear's Paw block. Trim excess fabric and batting. Clip all corners to the stitching line. Turn the table runner inside out and press. Hand-stitch the opening closed and quilt as desired.

Materials for 4 Place Mats

Yardage requirements are based on 42"-wide fabric unless otherwise stated.

1 yd. dark fabric (fabric A) for sampler blocks, toes and center squares in Bear's Paw blocks, and sashing

2 fat quarters medium fabric (fabrics B and C) for sampler blocks

2 fat quarters medium-dark fabric (fabric D) for sampler blocks

1 yd. light background fabric (fabric E)

1¼ yds. for backing

Four 19" x 19" pieces of batting

Cutting Directions for Place Mats

To best use your fabric, first cut all fabric pieces as listed below; then cut the fabrics for the sampler blocks as indicated on pages 7–19. All measurements include ¼"-wide seam allowances.

From fabric A, cut:
- 16 strips, each 2½" x 14½", for sashing
- 4 squares, each 2½" x 2½", for center squares of Bear's Paw blocks
- 4 rectangles, each 7" x 12", for toes in Bear's Paw blocks

From fabric E, cut:
- 16 rectangles, each 2½" x 6½", for Bear's Paw blocks
- 4 rectangles, each 7" x 12", for toes in Bear's Paw blocks
- 32 squares, each 2½" x 2½", for Bear's Paw blocks and sashing

Blocks for Place Mats

1. Make 4 each of the following sampler blocks: Friendship Star (page 9), Old Maid's Puzzle (page 10), Birds in Flight (page 12), and Railroad Crossing (page 17). Or choose your favorite sampler block and make all 4 of the place mats identical. If you use different sampler blocks from those shown, the yardage requirements may vary.

2. Following the instructions for "Bear's Paw Block" (page 7), construct 4 blocks. Use the 7" x 12" fabric A and fabric E rectangles to make the toes. Use 4 identical sampler blocks for each Bear's Paw block.

Assembly and Finishing for Place Mats

1. Join four 2½" x 14½" fabric A rectangles, four 2½" fabric E squares, and a Bear's Paw block.

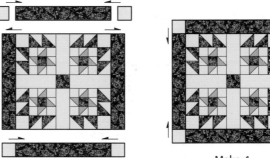

Make 4.

2. For each place mat, layer batting, backing, and the place mat top on your work surface, right sides together. Pin-baste the layers together and stitch ¼" from all edges, leaving a 5" opening on one side. Trim excess fabric and batting. Clip all corners to the stitching line. Turn the place mat right side out and press. Hand-stitch the opening closed and quilt as desired.

Peaches-and-Cream Porridge

By Maret Anderson.

This is a twin-size Bear's Paw sampler, set on point with coordinating pillow shams.

Finished Quilt Size: 69" x 94½"
Finished Pillow-Sham Size: 22½" x 28½"
Finished Block Size: 14" x 14"

Materials for Quilt and Pillow Shams

Yardage requirements are based on 42"-wide fabric unless otherwise stated.

2⅜ yds. medium fabric (fabric A) for outer border, sashing, and pillow shams

5 or more fat quarters of light, medium, and dark fabrics (fabric B) for sampler blocks and for toes in pillow-sham Bear's Paw blocks

1⅞ yds. dark fabric (fabric C) for star cornerstones, binding, and pillow shams

1⅔ yds. medium-dark fabric (fabric D) for toes in quilt Bear's Paw blocks, inner border, and pillow shams

3⅛ yds. light background fabric (fabric E) for quilt and pillow shams

7 yds. for backings of quilt and pillow shams

1⅓ yds. for lining on pillow sham

72" x 98" piece of batting for quilt

1⅓ yd. lightweight batting for pillow shams

2 standard-size bed pillows

Cutting for Quilt

To best use your fabric, cut all fabric pieces as listed below first; then cut the fabrics for the sampler blocks as indicated on pages 7–19. All measurements include ¼"-wide seam allowances.

From fabric A, cut:
- 24 strips, each 4½" x 14½", for sashing
- 8 strips, each 4½" x 42", for outer borders

From fabric B, cut:
- 6 squares, each 2½" x 2½", for center squares in Bear's Paw blocks

From fabric C, cut:
- 17 squares, each 4½" x 4½", for star centers
- 96 squares, each 2½" x 2½", for star points
- 8 strips, each 2¼" x 42", for binding

From fabric D, cut:
- 6 rectangles, each 7" x 12", for toes in Bear's Paw blocks
- 7 strips, each 2½" x 42", for inner border

From fabric E, cut:
- 2 squares, each 27" x 27"; cut the squares twice diagonally to make 8 side setting triangles (you will have 2 left over)
- 2 squares, each 17" x 17"; cut the squares once diagonally to make 4 corner setting triangles
- 2 squares, each 14½" x 14½", for alternate blocks
- 6 rectangles, each 7" x 12", for toes in Bear's Paw blocks
- 24 rectangles, each 2½" x 6½", for Bear's Paw blocks
- 24 squares, each 2½" x 2½", for Bear's Paw blocks

Blocks for Quilt

1. Make 4 each of the following sampler blocks: Churn Dash (page 8), Birds in Flight (page 12), Nine Patch (page 14), Sawtooth Star (page 15), Shoofly (page 16), and Railroad Crossing (page 17). In place of the 6 sampler block designs used here, you may substitute any of the sampler blocks found on pages 7–19 to make this quilt. Or choose your favorite sampler block and use it throughout the quilt, if desired. If you use different sampler blocks from those shown, the yardage requirements may vary.

2. Following the instructions for "Bear's Paw Block" (page 7), construct 6 blocks. Use the 7" x 12" fabric D and fabric E rectangles for the toes. Use 4 identical sampler blocks for each Bear's Paw block.

Star-Point Sashing

Draw a diagonal line from corner to corner on the wrong side of each 2½" fabric C square. Place a fabric C square on the upper corners of a 4½" x 14½" fabric A rectangle, right sides together. Sew on the marked lines. Trim ¼" from the stitching. Repeat with 2 more squares on the lower corners of the rectangle to make a star-point sashing strip.

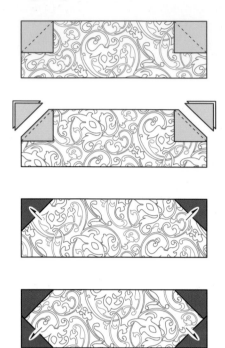

Make 24.

Assembly and Finishing for Quilt

1. Join a Bear's Paw block, 2 star-point sashing strips, and a 4½" fabric C square. Repeat with the 14½" fabric E alternate blocks.

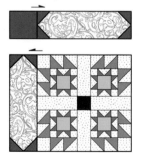

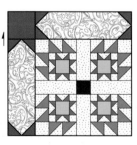

Make 6.

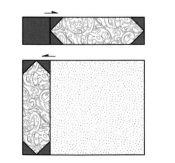
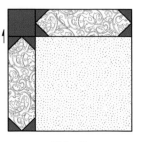

Make 2.

2. Join a 4½" fabric C square to the left edge of the remaining star-point sashing strips.

Make 8.

3. Arrange the blocks on point, add 4 of the star-point sashing units, and side triangles as shown.

4. Join the blocks, star-point sashing units, and side triangles in diagonal rows to make 2 halves.

5. Join 4 star-point sashing units; add a 4½" fabric C square to the end on the right.

6. Sew the long sashing strip between the 2 halves. Add the corner triangles last.

7. Trim the edges of the quilt ¼" away from all points, and square up corners if necessary.

8. Referring to "Adding Borders" (page 20), prepare the inner border strips and sew them to the top and bottom edges of the quilt top first; then sew the strips to the side edges. Repeat for the outer border.

9. Layer the pieced top with backing and batting; baste. Quilt as desired.

10. Bind the edges and add a label.

Cutting for Pillow Shams

From fabric B, cut:
- 2 rectangles, each 7" x 12", for toes in Bear's Paw blocks
- 2 squares, each 2½" x 2½", for center squares in Bear's Paw blocks

From fabric C, cut:
- 2 rectangles, each 3½" x 14½", for inner border of sham 1
- 2 rectangles, each 6½" x 20½", for inner border of sham 1
- 2 rectangles, each 1½" x 26½", for outer border of sham 2
- 2 rectangles, each 1½" x 22½", for outer border of sham 2

From fabric D, cut:
- 2 rectangles, each 3½" x 14½", for inner border of sham 2
- 2 rectangles, each 6½" x 20½", for inner border of sham 2
- 2 rectangles, each 1½" x 26½", for outer border of sham 1
- 2 rectangles, each 1½" x 22½", for outer border of sham 1

From fabric E, cut:
- 8 rectangles, each 2½" x 6½", for Bear's Paw blocks
- 8 squares, each 2½" x 2½", for Bear's Paw blocks
- 2 rectangles, each 7" x 12", for toes in Bear's Paw blocks

From the backing fabric, cut:
- 4 pieces, each 17½" x 22½"

From the lining fabric, cut:
- 2 pieces, each 22½" x 28½"

Blocks for Pillow Shams

1. Make 4 each of the following blocks: Birds in Flight (page 12) and Nine Patch (page 14). In place of the 2 sampler block designs used here, you may substitute any of the sampler blocks found on pages 7–19 to make this quilt. Or choose your favorite sampler block and use it throughout the quilt, if desired.

2. Following the instructions for "Bear's Paw Block" (page 7), construct 2 blocks. Use the 7" x 12" fabric B and fabric E rectangles for the toes. Use 4 identical sampler blocks for each Bear's Paw block.

Assembly and Finishing for Pillow Shams

1. Join the 3½" x 14½" and the 6½" x 20½" fabric C inner border rectangles to one of the Bear's Paw blocks. Repeat with fabric D inner border rectangles on the remaining Bear's Paw block.

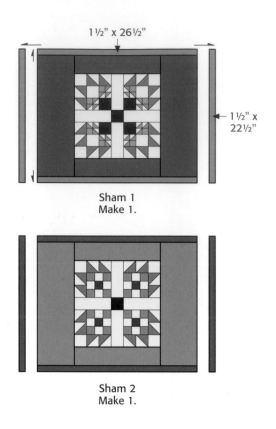

1½" x 26½"

1½" x 22½"

Sham 1
Make 1.

Sham 2
Make 1.

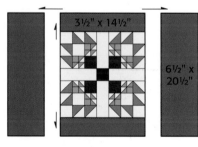

3½" x 14½"

6½" x 20½"

Sham 1
Make 1.

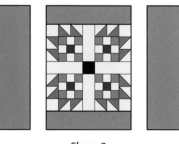

Sham 2
Make 1.

2. Join the 1½" x 26½" and the 1½" x 22½" contrasting outer border rectangles to each of the pillow shams.

3. Layer the lining, batting, and pillow-sham tops, wrong sides together. Quilt as desired. Trim the edges straight and corners square.

4. Turn under ¼" twice on the 22½" side of each backing piece. Stitch the fold.

5. Place a pillow-sham top on your work surface, right side up. Place a 17½" x 22½" backing piece, right side down, on the pillow sham, aligning the raw edges at one end. Place a second 17½" x 22½" backing piece on the pillow sham top in the same manner, overlapping the hemmed edges at the center.

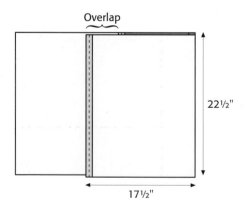

Overlap

22½"

17½"

6. Stitch all around the pillow, ¼" from the raw edges. Clip the corners and turn right side out. Stuff with a standard-size pillow.

Pattern for 1⅓" Finished Half-Square-Triangle Units

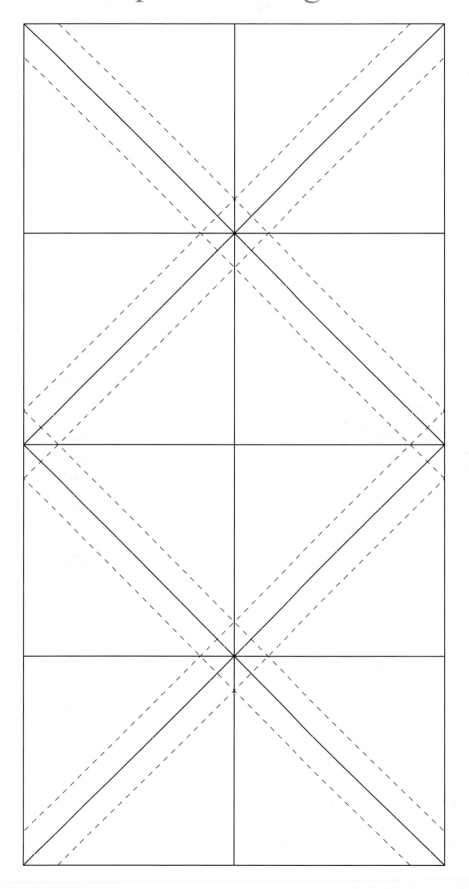

About the Author

Boyer Photography (Anchorage, Alaska)

Pat A. Syta started sewing when she was about twelve years old. In 1991 she began quilting when a friend she worked with talked her into taking her first quilting class. In the class, Pat was to make an eight-block beginning sampler, but eight blocks were not enough of a challenge, so Pat made an eighteen-block queen quilt, which she still sleeps under.

The quilting bug bit hard. Two years after her first class, Pat began teaching at a local shop in Anchorage, Alaska, where she still teaches today. Teaching beginners is her specialty, but she loves traveling, teaching all levels of students, and taking challenging classes herself. She does all of this in addition to her full-time job as an administrative assistant in one of the larger local elementary schools.

Pat's roots started in the very tiny town of Armstrong Creek, Wisconsin. After marrying her high school sweetheart and moving a few times with the military, Pat settled in Anchorage with her husband; they have lived there for the past twenty-five years. They have two sons and wonderful daughters-in-law. Dean is the expert who assists his mom with drafting the patterns she teaches, and Dale lives in Colorado and keeps tabs on Mom's quilting plans.

Pat is very active in the Valley Quilters Guild and is superintendent for the state fair quilting division. She also loves reading, organizing fun activities for friends and work, and of course, shopping. Trying to find time for quilting is always a challenge, but daydreaming of new projects in her studio is respite.